GABI'S IF/THEN GARDEN

written by Caroline Karanja
illustrated by Ben Whitehouse

PICTURE WINDOW BOOKS
a capstone imprint

Meet our coding creatives!

This is Adi. Adi likes arts and crafts. She spends most of her time coloring, playing music, and making things. Whenever she sees something new, she wonders how it came to be. She likes to say, "I wonder . . ."

This is Gabi. Gabi loves to read, play outside, and take care of her dog, Charlie. She is always curious about how things work. Whenever she sees something that needs fixing, she tries to find the best way to improve it. She often says, "What if . . .?"

Adi and Gabi make a great team!

Every spring the girls help their parents plant their gardens. They prepare the soil, choose which plants they'll grow, and plant the seeds.

If the weather is dry, **then** they water the plants.

If it rains, **then** they don't water the plants.

If weeds start to grow, **then** they pull them from the garden.

If a rabbit eats their plants, **then** they must start over!

Today Adi and Gabi are playing in Gabi's backyard.

"My mom said we could pick tomatoes," Gabi says. "Red tomatoes are ripe. Green ones aren't ripe yet. **If** a tomato is red, **then** put it in the basket. **If** the tomato is green, **then** leave it on the vine."

If/Then Statements

If/then examples are all around us: at home, at school, and in nature. Computers use if/then statements in their codes. A code is like a set of instructions for the computer to make it perform a task, such as showing a video or playing a game. In coding, if/then statements are called conditional statements. The "if" is the condition. Different conditions (or "ifs") will cause different outcomes (or "thens"). *If* something happens, *then* the computer does something.
Example:

If you press the number 3 key on the keyboard,
then a number 3 will show up on the screen.

If/thens are one of the ways we tell computers what to do.

"Can we water the plants?" Adi asks.

"Sure!" says Gabi. "**If** we turn this knob, **then** water will come out of the hose."

"And **if** we move the umbrella, **then** the plants will get some sun," Adi says.

That gives Gabi an idea. "Let's play the if/then game!"

"Only *if* you tell me what that is!" Adi says with a giggle.

"It's like Simon Says," Gabi explains, "but instead of Simon, the leader is called the Programmer. The follower is called the Computer. The Programmer gives the Computer commands. Commands are how a computer knows what to do. Like this: **If** the Programmer says *BOOP*, **then** the Computer says *BEEP*!"

"Boop!" Gabi shouts.

"Beep!" Adi shouts.

"Boop!" Gabi whispers.

"Beep!" Adi whispers.

"*Bonk!*" Gabi says.

Adi puts her hand over her mouth and shakes her head. "I can't say it!" she says. "That wasn't the right command!"

BOOP ➡ BEEP

"Good job following the commands, Computer!" Gabi says. "Now it's your turn to be the Programmer."

"OK," Adi says. "**If** the Programmer does a jumping jack, **then** the Computer does a cartwheel."

Adi does a jumping jack, and Gabi does a cartwheel. Adi does another jumping jack, but this time Gabi doesn't do a cartwheel. "Computer, what's wrong?" Adi asks.

"We have a bug in the code!" Gabi says. "To fix it, the Programmer has to ask the Computer questions."

"Hmmm," Adi says. "Are you hurt?"

Gabi shakes her head no.

"Are you tired?" Adi asks.

Bugs in the Code

Sometimes computers don't do what we expect them to do. The code is not working. Programmers have to try different things to figure out what's wrong. The problem is called a "bug," and fixing it is called "debugging." The programmer debugs the code to make it work again.

Gabi shakes her head again. She holds up her hands to give Adi a hint.

"Oh!" Adi says. Gabi's hands are covered in squashed tomato. "Are you dirty?"

Gabi nods her head yes and waves her messy hands in the air. "I cartwheeled right on top of a tomato!" she says.

Adi and Charlie help Gabi clean up.

"OK, let's try this again!" Adi says. She does a jumping jack, and Gabi does a cartwheel.

"The Computer is working again!" Gabi cheers. "The Programmer debugged the code—with Charlie's help!"

"The if/then game is fun!" Adi says.

"It's how computers know what to do," Gabi explains. "A programmer has to give it commands."

"Just like in the garden," Adi says.

"Right!" Gabi agrees.

Gabi and Adi are tired after a fun day in the garden.

Gabi says, "**If** your mom says it's all right, **then** you can come back tomorrow."

Adi says, "And **if** you give me some of those yummy pears, **then** my dad and I will make a pear tart to share with you tomorrow. . . ."

"OK!" Gabi says. "We make a good a team!"

Can you match these if/thens?

There are all sorts of fruits and vegetables in the garden. We can use them to create delicious things to eat! Use your finger to match each plant to the food it can make.

If you have . . .

then you can make . . .

Glossary

bug—a mistake in a computer program that keeps it from working correctly

code—one or more rules or commands to be carried out by a computer

command—an instruction that tells the computer to do something; many commands put together make up computer programs

computer—an electronic machine that can store and work with large amounts of information

condition—something that must be true in order for something to happen

conditional statement—statements that only run if something happens or is true; also called if/then statements

debug—to find and fix mistakes in programs

outcome—the result of a set of instructions

programmer—a person who writes code that can be run by a machine

Think in Code!

- Can you think of an if/then statement about what you might do on a Saturday if it's raining? What if it's sunny?
- Come up with an if/then statement about making your breakfast.
- Think of a computer game or program you use. What is an if/then condition that occurs while you play? What happens when you press a certain button? What happens when you win or lose the game?

About the Author

Caroline Karanja is a developer and designer who is on a mission to increase accessibility and sustainability through technology. She enjoys figuring out how things work and sharing this knowledge with others. She lives in Minneapolis.

This book is dedicated to my sister and friend Winnie —C. K.

Picture Window Books are published by Capstone
1710 Roe Crest Drive, North Mankato, Minnesota 56003
www.mycapstone.com

Library of Congress Cataloging-in-Publication data is available on the Library of
Congress website.

978-1-5158-3445-8 (paper over board)
978-1-5158-2745-0 (library hardcover)
978-1-5158-2749-8 (paperback)
978-1-5158-2753-5 (eBook PDF)

Summary: Two friends explore if/then statements and
how they are used in computer coding, as well as
in real-life applications, such as gardening.

Editor: Kristen Mohn
Designer: Kay Fraser
Design Element: Shutterstock/Arcady

Printed and bound in the United States of America.
PA021